Let's Always...

Promises to Make Love Last

Susan Newman

A Perigee Book

A Perigee Book
Published by The Berkley Publishing Group
200 Madison Avenue
New York, NY 10016

Copyright © 1995 by Susan Newman

Book design by Joseph Perez

Cover design by James R. Harris

Cover and text illustrations © 1995 by Marika Hahn

First edition: February 1995

Published simultaneously in Canada.

Library of Congress Cataloging-in-Publication Data
Newman, Susan.
    Let's always— / Susan Newman. —1st Perigee ed.
        p.   cm.
    ISBN 0-399-51901-7 (paper : alk. paper)
    1. Love—Miscellanea. 2. Marriage—Miscellanea. 3. Man-woman
relationships—Miscellanea.   I. Title.
HQ801.N48   1995
306.7—dc20   94-16788
                                                    CIP

Printed in the United States of America

10 9 8 7 6 5 4 3 2 1

This book is printed on acid-free paper.

$\mathcal{T}$o the men I have loved and who
have loved me; for it requires
give-and-take to fuel the feelings that
are the very heart of love.

Contents

$\mathcal{I}$ Love You Because . . .

* my heart beats faster when I'm with you.

* you say you love me at least once a day.

* you're not afraid to show affection in public.

* I feel comfortable with you.

———

$\mathcal{I}$ Love You Because . . .

* you hear me out when I complain.

* you anticipate my needs.

* you smother me with kisses.

* you listen when I brag about my

accomplishments.

$\mathcal{I}$ Love You Because . . .

* you make me feel young and carefree.

* you play tennis with me although

    I'm not very good.

* you look at me with love in your eyes.

* you like the things I like.

I Love You Because . . .

* you bring out the passion in me.

* you really understand me.

* you say what's on your mind.

* I know I can come to you

with any problem.

———

I Love You Because . . .

* your intentions are always good.

* you order one dessert and two forks.

* you remember me in special ways even

    when it's *not* a special occasion.

* we fit together perfectly.

I Love You Because . . .

* our love is pure.

* you care about my family, especially

    my parents.

* you let your emotions run free.

* you're considerate and kind.

$\mathcal{I}$ Love You Because . . .

* you're caring and sensitive.

* you make time for me.

* you do the unexpected.

* you stay with me in uncomfortable

   situations.

9

$\mathcal{I}$ Love You Because . . .

* you're tender and tough.

* you're generous.

* you're fun to be with.

* you find the best solutions to

  complicated problems.

10

$\mathscr{I}$ Love You Because ...

* you notice my new hairstyle.

* you make me feel secure

  and powerful.

* you support the causes I believe in.

* you tell me I'm the light of your life.

$\mathscr{I}$ Love You Because . . .

* you are the light of my life.

* you love and adore me.

* you keep me grounded.

* you look on the bright side.

$\mathcal{I}$ Love You Because . . .

* you plan our evenings perfectly.

* you always desire me.

* you're a good friend and a good lover.

* you share your feelings.

———

13

I Love You Because . . .

* you cheer me up when I feel down.

* you don't take advantage of my love.

* I know I can count on you if I'm in trouble.

* you make the world a happier place for me.

$\mathcal{I}$ Love You Because . . .

* you encourage me to be my best.

* you ask my advice on what you're wearing.

* you say flattering things about me to others.

* you have unending spirit.

—◦—

$\mathscr{I}$ Love You Because ...

* you ask nicely when you want something done.

* we are able to communicate without words.

* you don't try to prove that you're the better

   athlete or cook.

* I can never get enough of you.

$\mathcal{I}$ Love You Because . . .

* you calm me when I'm distraught.
* you read in another room if I want
  to sleep.
* you're open and honest.
* you have infinite patience.

———

$\mathcal{I}$ Love You Because . . .

* you're always willing to compromise.

* you make me feel wonderful.

* it's thrilling to be with you.

* you keep your promises.

—◆—

$\mathscr{I}$ Love You Because . . .

* we have a good time together.

* you remember and always want to celebrate

our first date.

* you even remember the day we met.

19

$\mathcal{I}$ Love You Because . . .

* you are the center of my life.

* you run the bathwater for me.

* you laugh at my jokes.

* I know you so well I can finish

  your thoughts.

I Love You Because . . .

* you respect me.

* I like your approach to life.

* you protect me.

* when you give me a gift, you take

  the time to wrap it.

—◁▷—

$\mathscr{I}$ Love You Because . . .

* when I'm dieting, you don't

  eat dessert.

* you ask my opinion.

* you tell me I'm attractive.

$\mathscr{I}$ Love You Because . . .

* you hold my hand when we walk.

* you're truly genuine.

* you take care of me when I'm not

  feeling well.

$\mathcal{I}$ Love You Because . . .

* you buy the gifts I like.

* you worry if I'm sad.

* you're proud of me and say so.

* you blow kisses across the room.

$\mathcal{I}$ Love You Because . . .

* you read me parts of the newspaper

you know I'm interested in.

* you hold me after the music stops.

* loving you makes life worthwhile.

I Promise

Always To...

$\mathcal{I}$ Promise Always To ...

* treasure you.

* keep a photograph of us on my desk.

* call if I am going to be late.

* astound you with the depth of my feeling.

—⁂—

$\mathscr{I}$ Promise Always To . . .

* make you my one and only.

* encourage and support you.

* meet you at the airport after a business trip.

* be overjoyed to see you when you've been away.

———

$\mathscr{I}$ Promise Always To . . .

* remember our anniversary.

* be affectionate.

* view life with you as my special privilege.

* build your confidence.

$\mathscr{I}$ Promise Always To . . .

* share my private thoughts and fears.

* cherish our time together.

* try to understand what makes you tick.

* listen to your political views even if I disagree.

———

$\mathcal{I}$ Promise Always To . . .

* look the other way when you behave foolishly.

* be interesting so you don't get bored with me.

* resist the temptation to have the last word.

* flirt with you.

33

$\mathcal{I}$ Promise Always To ...

* compliment you.

* care about your well-being as much as I care
  about my own.

* make changes if they will create a more
  pleasant life together.

$\mathcal{I}$ Promise Always To . . .

* tell you if an outfit doesn't match.

* use the presents you give me.

* consider our commitment deep

  and permanent.

* be on your side.

$\mathscr{I}$ Promise Always To . . .

* notice when you seem upset.

* use holidays as an excuse to make
  a big fuss over you.

* be considerate of the important
  people in your life.

36

ℐ Promise Always To . . .

* say thank you whenever you go out

  of your way for me.
* marvel at the magic we make.
* remind you how smart you are.
* trust you.

⁓

I Promise Always To . . .

* let you know how funny

I think you are.

* say only the nicest things about

you to others.

* leave you alone when you're

swamped with work.

$\mathscr{I}$ Promise Always To . . .

* tell you how sexy you are to me.

* make you my singular passion.

* tell you you're the best as often

   as you can stand to hear it.

* help you find your lost keys,

   wallet or gloves.

$\mathcal{I}$ Promise Always To . . .

* start each day with a kiss and kind words.

* be your Valentine.

* mark special occasions with a gift

or flowers.

$\mathscr{I}$ Promise Always To . . .

* keep cutting remarks to myself.

* remember what you tell me.

* discuss my hopes and dreams with you.

* be the love of your life.

I Promise Always To . . .

* carry your picture in my wallet.

* ask for help when I need it.

* pledge my love out loud.

* insist on a good-night kiss—

    or two or three.

I Promise Always To ...

* give in whenever possible.

* give you moral support.

* be gracious to your friends

  and coworkers.

* tell others how much I love you.

43

I Promise Always To . . .

* be your treat on Halloween.

* call you first with good news.

* give you a second chance.

* cheer for your team.

$\mathcal{I}$ Promise Always To . . .

* keep a photo album of the memorable

   times we share.

* be empathetic.

* try very hard to resolve our differences.

—⁂—

$\mathscr{I}$ Promise Always To . . .

* ask about your work.

* be your old—and new—flame.

* share my lottery winnings.

* listen to your office problems.

* be sensual.

I Promise Always To . . .

* confide in you.

* steer clear of issues I know upset you.

* speak to your parents regularly and

  with interest.

* be receptive to your ideas and suggestions.

$\mathscr{I}$ Promise Always To . . .

* put the cap on the toothpaste.

* respect your "body clock" and energy level.

* think about you when we are apart.

* admit when I'm wrong.

* call home every night when I'm out of town.

$\mathcal{I}$ Promise Always To . . .

* be enthusiastic about your every success.

* look my best even while painting a room or
  cleaning the garage.

* be an emotional anchor when you are
  faced with failure.

$\mathscr{I}$ Promise Always To . . .

* go along on important appointments
  with the doctor.
* stay in the hospital with you.
* pass along the compliments I hear
  about you.

$\mathscr{I}$ Promise Always To . . .

* sit close when we watch television.

* caress you when you least expect it.

* honor your privacy.

* follow you wherever your job takes you.

* look into your eyes when you speak to me.

$\mathcal{I}$ Promise Always To . . .

* relay all messages, even ones that may

   ruin our plans.

* accept criticism as graciously as I can.

* read the menu if you've forgotten

   your glasses.

* make you look good in front of other people.

$\mathcal{I}$ Promise Always To . . .

* boast about your latest accomplishment.

* be devoted to you.

* appreciate the small things you do for me.

* work hard at maintaining the spark

   in our relationship.

* love you for better or worse—for life.

I Promise

Never To . . .

$\mathcal{I}$ Promise Never To . . .

* let you down if I can prevent it.

* suppress my desire to be with you.

* leave your gas tank empty.

* leave a space between us on the

couch or in bed.

$\mathcal{I}$ Promise Never To . . .

* try to change you. I know I can't.

* assume you will always love me.

* become defensive.

* give up on our love.

* forget your birthday.

I Promise Never To . . .

* plan an outing or event without
  checking with you.
* leave a ring in the bathtub.
* read or watch television
  during meals.

59

$\mathcal{I}$ Promise Never To . . .

* discuss past involvements.

* lose my sense of humor.

* take you and the things you do for me

  for granted.

* be disagreeable in front of others,

  even if I am annoyed with you.

———

I Promise Never To . . .

* place our happiness in jeopardy.

* be selfish where you are concerned.

* keep secrets from you.

* show your baby pictures if it

  embarrasses you.

* crowd you.

$\mathcal{I}$ Promise Never To . . .

* say hurtful things during

  a heated debate.

* harp on old mistakes.

* question the intangibles that bind us.

* yell at you.

$\mathcal{I}$ Promise Never To . . .

* purchase expensive items without
  consulting you.

* doubt your word.

* talk to you before you've had coffee
  in the morning.

—◈—

$\mathcal{I}$ Promise Never To . . .

* make light of our friendship.

* harbor a grudge.

* take advantage of your good nature.

* divulge a secret you have

   entrusted to me.

⟨≈⟩

I Promise Never To . . .

* make comments that will ignite or

  fuel a disagreement.

* go to bed angry.

* ridicule you when people are around.

* belittle you when we're alone.

$\mathcal{I}$ Promise Never To . . .

* withhold sex to win an argument or

    to get my way.

* do anything that would harm

    our relationship.

* approach you with ulterior motives.

I Promise Never To . . .

* go through your personal papers or listen

  to your private conversations.

* keep you waiting.

* correct your grammar in front

  of others.

$\mathcal{I}$ Promise Never To . . .

* use up all the hot water.

* second-guess you.

* tell anyone your age if you are

   sensitive about it.

―――

I Promise Never To . . .

* be jealous.

* give you reasons to worry about

   our relationship.

* stop loving you.

—⦿—

Whenever

I Can, I'll . . .

Whenever I Can, I'll . . .

* smooth the path for you.

* splurge on an extravagant treat for us.

* remind you how important you are to me.

* touch you and hold you.

Whenever I Can, I'll . . .

* do more than what's called for.

* cook and eat the fish, duck, rabbit or

    deer you catch.

* rub your back or give you a massage.

* warm up the bed.

*W*henever I Can, I'll . . .

* clean out the inside of your car.

* find new restaurants to try and

  places to go.

* put your preferences before my own.

* keep nagging to the bare minimum.

$\mathcal{W}$henever I Can, I'll . . .

* buy you a gift for no reason.

* tickle you affectionately.

* start a pillow fight.

* help you pack for a business

  trip or vacation.

Whenever I Can, I'll . . .

* warm the car on a wintery morning.

* swallow my pride to avoid

   an argument.

* allow my whimsical side to show.

* share my bubble bath with you.

*W*henever I Can, I'll . . .

* keep the kitchen stocked with our
  favorite foods.
* call for no reason, just to touch base,
  or say I miss you.
* keep the house quiet if you're trying
  to work.

$\mathcal{W}$henever I Can, I'll . . .

* experiment with new recipes so meals
  are more interesting.
* make the phone calls you would rather
  not make.
* discover something new and wonderful
  about you . . . and tell you what it is.

$\mathscr{W}$henever I Can, I'll . . .

* hole up with you for the weekend.

* buy the Sunday papers before

  you get up.

* report the day's pluses before

  delving into its disasters.

$\mathscr{W}$henever I Can, I'll ...

* leave a message to make you smile

    or feel good.

* do more than my share of the

    household chores.

* help you with your aging or sickly parents.

$\mathcal{W}$henever I Can, I'll . . .

* rent an isolated cabin in the woods for us.

* nap with you in the afternoon.

* attend your business functions willingly.

* find an excuse for us to open a bottle of

   champagne and celebrate.

—⚬—

*W*henever I Can, I'll . . .

* do things without waiting to be asked.

* overlook the small things you do

    that annoy me.

* remove the snow and ice from

    your windshield.

Whenever I Can, I'll . . .

* take care of the things that drive you crazy.

* fill a Christmas stocking for you.

* buy gifts for your father and mother.

* bring you a cup of coffee first thing
   in the morning.

*W*henever I Can, I'll . . .

* leave work at the office so our

    evenings can be relaxed.

* offer to fill your plate at a buffet.

* follow your advice.

* leave a note that expresses my love.

$\mathcal{T}$o Keep Our Love Strong, Let's . . .

* practice kissing.

* go dancing.

* pretend that we're the only

   two people on earth.

* go ice skating or sledding.

$\mathcal{T}$o Keep Our Love Strong, Let's . . .

* keep our love versatile.

* find a romantic spot to call our own.

* go off our diets and eat something

   sexy and sinful.

* accept each other's quirks.

To Keep Our Love Strong, Let's . . .

* toast each other when the mood hits us.

* have a quiet picnic by ourselves.

* rent a tandem bike.

* remove as much stress from our

   lives as we can.

—

$\mathscr{T}$o Keep Our Love Strong, Let's . . .

* have breakfast in bed.

* return to the site of our first date.

* go mountain climbing and sleep under the stars.

* say something loving once a day.

$\mathcal{T}$o Keep Our Love Strong, Let's . . .

* make the most of our time together.

* walk barefoot on a warm, rainy day.

* learn to play bridge or chess.

* find time to sit together doing nothing.

$\mathcal{T}$o Keep Our Love Strong, Let's . . .

* light a candle instead of a lamp.

* decide to take up bird watching.

* give each other impromptu hugs and kisses.

* watch the sunrise together.

$\mathcal{T}$o Keep Our Love Strong, Let's . . .

* watch the sunset together.

* reaffirm our commitment every so often.

* work out together.

* linger over coffee after dinner.

$\mathscr{T}$o Keep Our Love Strong, Let's . . .

* paddle a canoe.

* take long, leisurely walks.

* get away for one vacation or more a year.

* sit quietly by the lake or ocean.

$\mathcal{T}$o Keep Our Love Strong, Let's . . .

* drop everything and see a romantic movie.

* eat from the same bag or bowl of popcorn.

* go to a dude ranch.

* take a walk in the bright moonlight.

$\mathcal{T}$o Keep Our Love Strong, Let's . . .

* make a joint wish on the first star
  we see at night.
* flatter each other frequently.
* take home a provocative video for
  private viewing.
* ride a river in inner tubes.

$\mathcal{T}$o Keep Our Love Strong, Let's . . .

* feed each other strawberries and

   whipped cream.

* be suggestive.

* attend an outdoor concert.

* plant a shrub or tree to mark

   each anniversary.

$\mathcal{T}$o Keep Our Love Strong, Let's . . .

* kiss underwater.

* do something reckless together.

* curl up under a blanket to watch a movie.

* eat by candlelight now and then.

To Keep Our Love Strong, Let's . . .

* take ballroom dance lessons.

* find a hill and roll down it together.

* bury each other in sand at the beach.

* apply one another's suntan lotion.

$\mathcal{T}$o Keep Our Love Strong, Let's . . .

* celebrate the small—as well as the large—
achievements in our lives.
* light a fire in the fireplace for a
romantic glow.
* read sexy or tender love passages aloud
to each other.

$\mathcal{T}$o Keep Our Love Strong, Let's . . .

* plan lunchtime getaways.

* save special wineglasses just

 for the two of us.

* buy books for each other.

* act silly whenever we can.

* buy candy in a heart-shaped box.

$\mathcal{T}$o Keep Our Love Strong, Let's . . .

* find time to talk about our relationship.

* pretend we won a million dollars.

* stay on the beach after everyone else

   has gone.

* be sentimental on Valentine's Day.

$\mathscr{T}$o Keep Our Love Strong, Let's . . .

* bring home a balloon that says

    "I Love You."

* mail an "I Love You" card or note

    to the office.

* go strawberry picking.

To Keep Our Love Strong, Let's . . .

* ride through the Tunnel of Love

at an amusement park.

* swing in a hammock together.

* cut down our social obligations to have

more time to be with each other.

$\mathscr{T}$o Keep Our Love Strong, Let's . . .

* ride a seesaw for the fun of it.

* have dinner in bed.

* carve our initials and the date in one

   of our trees.

* play "our" song frequently.

$\mathscr{T}_{o}$ Keep Our Love Strong, Let's . . .

* share a hot fudge sundae.

* walk along a deserted beach in early morning
   or at dusk.

* ride bicycles . . . and wait when one of us
   can't keep the pace.

* prepare dinner and do the dishes together.

$\mathcal{T}$o Keep Our Love Strong, Let's . . .

* grant each other some personal freedom.

* roast marshmallows in the fireplace.

* sleep in front of a crackling fire.

* hire a masseuse.

* celebrate nothing more than the joy of

  being together.

$\mathcal{T}$o Keep Our Love Strong, Let's . . .

* hike through the woods in early spring.

* go skinny-dipping.

* share pleasant childhood memories.

* go apple picking every fall.

𝒯o Keep Our Love Strong, Let's . . .

* plan our goals individually and as a couple.

* switch sides of the bed.

* shower together.

* not spend our lives at work.

To Keep Our Love Strong, Let's . . .

* make sure we both love a painting

before we buy it.

* do only the things that make us laugh . . .

that make us feel glad.

$\mathcal{T}$o Keep Our Love Strong, Let's . . .

* be sensitive to each other's needs.

* relive the excellent times we have had.

* talk about what we'll do when we're

   old and gray.

And, Let's Always...

And, Let's Always . . .

* believe in each other.

* share our victories.

* hold hands.

* be thankful that we found each other.

$\mathcal{A}$nd, Let's Always . . .

* keep the flame of love alive.

* make intimate rituals a part of our life.

* make real plans for a real date even

  when we've been together for years.

* be generous with compliments.

$\mathcal{A}$nd, Let's Always . . .

* be partners in every sense.

* tell one another if we feel ignored.

* linger in bed together longer than

    we should.

* love each other more than words can say.

$\mathcal{A}$nd, Let's Always . . .

* celebrate the milestones that mark

  our relationship.

* say amorous things to one another.

* consider ourselves a pair.

* build tradition into our life.

$\mathscr{A}$nd, Let's Always . . .

* have peaceful, romantic dinners.

* make our love our top priority.

* be spontaneous.

* make time for lingering kisses

  instead of quick pecks.

And, Let's Always . . .

* feel free with one another.

* respect each other's wishes.

* rub noses.

* be a bit mysterious.

* savor the intensity of our love.

$\mathscr{A}$nd, Let's Always . . .

* kiss hello and good-bye no matter

  how rushed we are.

* try to be in good humor when we're together.

* be sure we know how to reach each other

  during the day.

*A*nd, Let's Always . . .

* speak up when our feelings are hurt.

* consider ourselves each other's

   better half.

* be playful.

* be passionate.

And, Let's Always . . .

* be kind.

* be polite.

* listen to music we both enjoy.

* make intimacy standard operating

    procedure.

---

*A*nd, Let's Always . . .

* kiss and make up.

* forgive and move on.

* address each other by our pet names.

* gaze deeply into each other's eyes.

———

$\mathcal{A}$nd, Let's Always . . .

* dream of our future.

* keep in mind that we're a team and

we belong together.

* reconnect at night.

$\mathcal{A}$nd, Let's Always . . .

* capture our memorable moments on film.

* imagine our love is as powerful as

  Romeo and Juliet's.

* be compassionate.

* listen—really listen—to each other.

—

$\mathcal{A}$nd, Let's Always . . .

* remember that little things mean a lot.

* inquire about each other's day.

* talk and listen in balanced proportions.

* cocoon alone—just you and me—as often
  and for as long as possible.

*A*nd, Let's Always . . .

* help one another through trying periods.

* move heaven and earth to make each other happy.

* look for the lighter side of our disagreements.

* think we have it all.

* be grateful we have each other for companionship.

———

*A*nd, Let's Always . . .

* settle our differences quickly so they don't

  have a chance to come between us.

* bring home souvenirs from our travels so

  we can reminisce.

* share personal thoughts and fantasies.

131

*A*nd, Let's Always . . .

* feed each other now and again.

* maintain our mutual admiration society.

* reserve the bedroom for romance, not work.

* be a caring twosome.

*A*nd, Let's Always . . .

* hope luck is on our side.

* act young and foolish.

* sing together, even if we're off key.

* preserve our emotional closeness.

———

$\mathcal{A}$nd, Let's Always . . .

* work at making our love perfect.

* prefer being with one another

   above all others.

* remember I'm yours and you are mine.

* deem ours the greatest love of all.

———

*A*nd, Let's Always . . .

* be in each other's hearts.

* cherish our happiness.

* be ourselves.

* be together.

* believe the best is yet to come.

About the Author

Susan Newman is the author of many parenting books, among them *Parenting an Only Child* and *Little Things Long Remembered: Making Your Children Feel Special Every Day.* She is also the author of books for children and teenagers, including the best-selling *Never Say Yes to a Stranger* and *It Won't Happen to Me: True Stories of Teen Alcohol and Drug Abuse.* She lives with her family in New Jersey.